D1250981

7

DATE DUE

Science Tools

Telescopes

by Adele Richardson

Consultant:
Dr. Ronald Browne
Associate Professor of Elementary Education
Minnesota State University, Mankato

Capstone
press

Mankato, Minnesota

First Facts is published by Capstone Press
151 Good Counsel Drive, P.O. Box 669, Mankato, Minnesota 56002
www.capstonepress.com

Library of Congress Cataloging-in-Publication Data
Richardson, Adele, 1966–
    Telescopes / by Adele Richardson.
    p. cm.—(First facts. Science tools)
    Summary: Introduces the function, parts, and uses of telescopes, and provides
instructions for two activities that demonstrate how a telescope works.
    Includes bibliographical references and index.
    ISBN 0-7368-2518-5 (hardcover)
    1. Telescopes—Juvenile literature. [1. Telescopes.] I. Title. II. Series.
QB88.R34 2004
522'.2—dc22
                                        2003013402

Editorial Credits
Christopher Harbo, editor; Juliette Peters, designer; Erin Scott, SARIN Creative, illustrator;
    Deirdre Barton, photo researcher; Eric Kudalis, product planning editor

Photo Credits
Capstone Press/Gary Sundermeyer, 1, 4–5, 6, 9, 11, 12, 16, 17
Capstone Press/GEM Photo Studio/Dan Delaney, cover
Corbis/Jim Craigmyle, 7; Roger Ressmeyer, 13, 14, 15
Photodisc/StockTrek, 18, 20

1 2 3 4 5 6 09 08 07 06 05 04

Table of Contents

The Planetarium

Mrs. Serrano's students are visiting a **planetarium**. Planetariums are places where people learn about planets and stars. They also learn about the tools used to study outer space. The planetarium guide shows the students how to use a telescope.

 Fun Fact:
A planetarium has a curved ceiling. The ceiling is like a movie screen. Pictures of stars and planets are shown on the ceiling.

What Is a Telescope?

Telescopes are tools that help people see faraway things. Telescopes use lenses or mirrors to gather light. They gather more light than our eyes can collect.

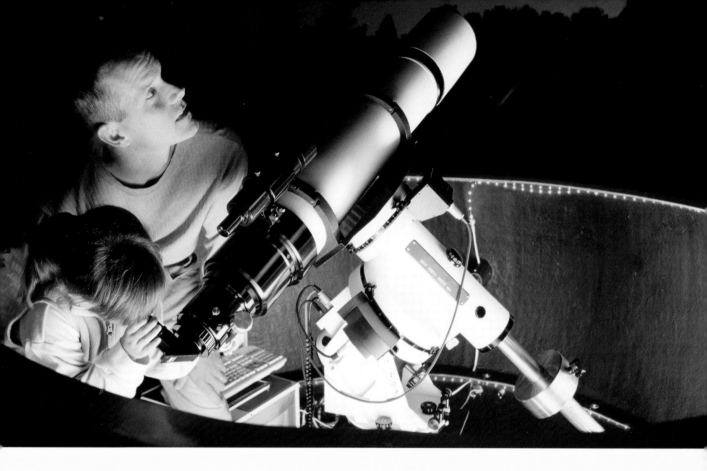

Telescopes **magnify** the light collected to make objects look bigger. Telescopes can be used at night to collect light from distant stars.

Fun Fact:
Some people use reflecting telescopes. These telescopes use mirrors instead of lenses to gather light.

Parts of a Telescope

A **refracting telescope** is a long tube with lenses. A **focus knob** in front of the eyepiece helps make images clear. A finder scope on top of the telescope helps aim the telescope. A **mount** holds the telescope steady. The telescope can turn and tilt on the mount.

 Fun Fact:
In 1608, Hans Lippershey made the first telescope with lenses in Holland.

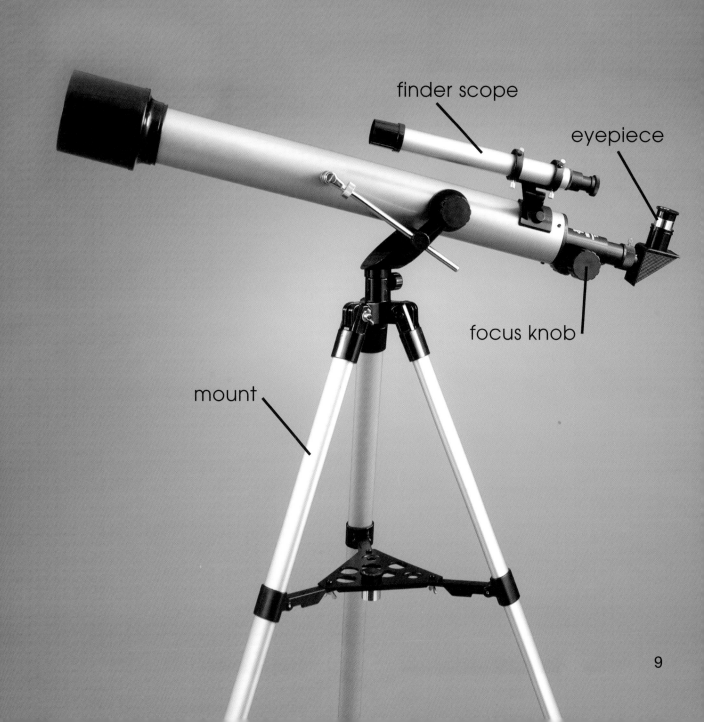

finder scope

eyepiece

focus knob

mount

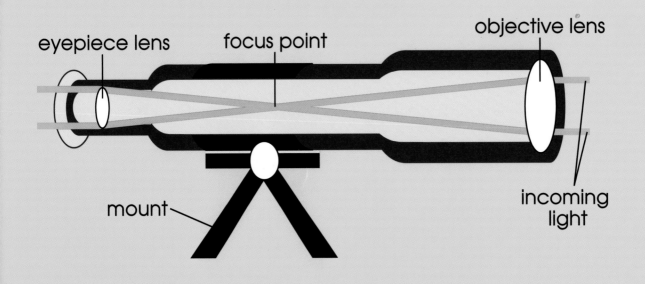

eyepiece lens

focus point

objective lens

incoming light

mount

Telescope Lenses

Refracting telescopes use curved lenses. An objective lens collects light. The light bends to a bright point. An eyepiece lens magnifies the light.

This student is looking through the telescope's eyepiece. He turns the focus knob as he looks through the eyepiece.

Telescopes in School

Students use telescopes to learn about the Moon, planets, and stars. These students are learning how to look for stars in **constellations**.

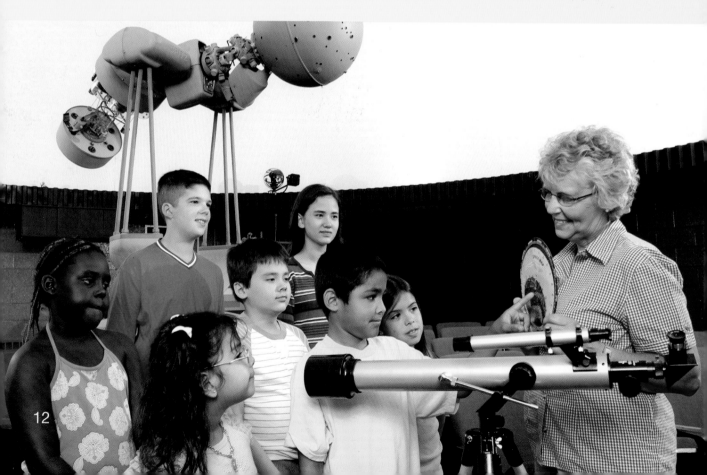

A constellation is a group of stars. These stars form shapes. Some shapes look like animals or people. The constellation Orion looks like a man.

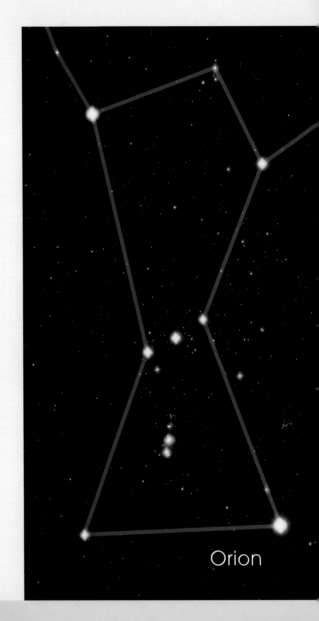

Orion

Other Uses for Telescopes

Astronomers use telescopes to study outer space. These scientists have discovered planets, stars, comets, and asteroids with telescopes.

Many astronomers work in
observatories. Observatories have
large telescopes to look far into space.

Fun Fact:
The largest observatory in the world
is on Mount Kea in Hawaii.

Test the World around You

Aiming a telescope takes practice. Small objects in the sky can be hard to find. Many people practice aiming their telescopes. They aim at objects at the top of water towers or other tall structures.

Try It!

What You Need

telescope
water tower (or other tall structure)

What You Do

1. Find an area where you can see a water tower in the distance.
2. Look at the water tower without the telescope. Find a target near the top of the water tower. The target could be a letter, a light, or the pointed top of the tower.
3. Set up your telescope. Aim it at the water tower.
4. Look through the finder scope on the telescope. Change the direction and tilt of the telescope until the target is in the center of the finder scope.
5. Look through the eyepiece lens. Can you see your target? If not, repeat steps 2 and 3.
6. Once you see your target, turn the focus knob until you see the target clearly.

What Did They Learn?

Mrs. Serrano's students learned how to use a telescope to look at the Moon. Can you find these Moon features with a telescope?

Crater Plato

Crater Aristotle

Crater Copernicus

Sea of Crises

Sea of Tranquillity

Crater Grimaldi

Sea of Clouds

Crater Tycho

Try It!

What You Need

Moon photo on page 18   telescope
piece of paper   full Moon
pencil

What You Do

1. Look at the labeled picture of the Moon on page 18.
2. On a piece of paper, write the names of each feature.
3. Carefully set up your telescope. Use the finder scope to aim the telescope at the full Moon.
4. Look through the eyepiece lens of the telescope. Turn the focus knob until you can see the Moon clearly.
5. Find each feature, one at a time. Each time you find a feature, place a checkmark next to it on your paper.

Did you find all of the features with your telescope? Were some of the features harder to find than others? Try looking at some of the stars in the night sky. You may even see the planets Saturn or Mars.

Fun Fact:
The same side of the Moon always faces Earth.

Telescopes allow people to look back in time. A light-year is the distance light travels in one year. The Orion Nebula in the constellation Orion is about 2,000 light-years away. People who look at the nebula today are seeing what it looked like 2,000 years ago.

What Do You Think?

1. Why is the mount an important part of a telescope?

2. Why do telescopes have curved lenses?

3. A telescope is a tool used to study planets and stars. Where do people use telescopes at work?

4. Telescopes gather more light than our eyes can collect. What helps telescopes gather more light?

Glossary

constellation (kon-stuh-LAY-shuhn)—a group of stars that forms a shape

focus knob (FOH-kuhss NOB)—a round dial on a telescope that turns to make images look clear

magnify (MAG-nuh-fye)—to make something look bigger than it really is

mount (MOUNT)—a stand with three legs that holds a telescope

observatory (uhb-ZUR-vuh-tor-ee)—a building with telescopes and other scientific tools for studying stars and planets

planetarium (plan-uh-TAIR-ee-uhm)—a building where pictures of stars and planets are shown on a curved ceiling

refracting telescope (ri-FRAK-ting TEL-uh-skope)—a telescope that uses curved lenses to collect and magnify light

Read More

Bullock, Linda. *Looking through a Telescope.* Rookie Read-About Science. New York: Children's Press, 2003.

Roza, Greg. *The Incredible Story of Telescopes.* A Kid's Guide to Incredible Technology. New York: Rosen, 2004.

Internet Sites

FactHound offers a safe, fun way to find Internet sites related to this book. All of the sites on FactHound have been researched by our staff.

Here's how:
1. Visit *www.facthound.com*
2. Type in this special code **0736825185** for age-appropriate sites. Or enter a search word related to this book for a more general search.
3. Click on the **Fetch It** button.

FactHound will fetch the best sites for you!

Index

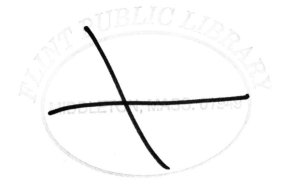